TENEMENT

TENEMENT

Immigrant Life on the Lower East Side

RAYMOND BIAL

Houghton Mifflin Company Boston 2002

Special thanks to the Lower East Side Tenement Museum, 97 Orchard Street, New York, New York 10002. Telephone: 212-431-0233.

www.houghtonmifflinbooks.com

Book design by Lisa Diercks
The text of this book is set in Filosofia.

Library of Congress Cataloging-in-Publication Data

Bial, Raymond.
Tenement : immigrant life on the Lower East Side / Raymond Bial.
p. cm.
Summary: Presents a view of New York City's tenements during the peak years of foreign immigration, discussing living conditions, laws pertaining to tenements, and the occupations of their residents. Includes bibliographical references.
ISBN 0-618-13849-8 (hardcover)
1. Poor—New York (State)—New York—Juvenile literature. 2. Immigrants—New York (State)—New York—Juvenile literature. 3. Tenement houses—New York (State)—New York—Juvenile literature. 4. Lower East Side (New York, N.Y.)—Social conditions—Juvenile literature. [1. Poor—New York (State)—New York. 2. Immigrants—New York (State)—New York. 3. Tenement houses. 4. New York (N.Y.)—Social conditions. 5. New York (N.Y.)—History.] I. Title.
HV4046.N6 B53 2002   307.76'4'097471—dc21   2002000407

Photo Credits
The photographs on the following pages are from *How the Other Half Lives* by Jacob Riis, and they have been graciously provided by the Museum of the City of New York: viii, 11, 15, 16, 18, 19, 21, 24, 33, 34, 44. John Seder, a native New Yorker, made the photograph that appears on page 45.
All other photographs are by the author.

Printed in Singapore
TWP 10 9 8 7 6 5 4 3 2 1

THIS BOOK IS DEDICATED TO MY GRANDPARENTS AND THOSE OF MY wife, Linda, all of whom came to America from other countries—Germany, Poland, Lithuania, Slovenia, Hungary, and Italy—in the early years of the twentieth century. Fearful yet hopeful, impoverished yet hardworking, they arrived at Ellis Island and other ports of entry. Like other immigrants, they lived for a time in tenements and boarding houses in poor neighborhoods. Like other immigrants, they sought a better life for themselves, their children, and their grandchildren. It was a lifelong task that was admirably achieved.

ACKNOWLEDGMENTS

I WOULD LIKE TO THANK THE LOWER EAST SIDE TENEMENT MUSEUM for allowing me to photograph at their site. I am grateful to the City Museum of New York, which provided a number of striking photographs. I would also like to thank my friend and fellow photographer John Seder for his help with this project. I offer my deepest appreciation for my daughter Anna, who accompanied me on the photo shoot to New York City. Without her assistance I would not have been able to take the photographs that appear in this book.

After a hazardous journey across the Atlantic Ocean from her home in Italy, this woman and her baby found themselves trapped in poverty in a small tenement on Jersey Street around 1889.

FROM THE EARLY 1800S TO THE 1930S, MILLIONS OF IMMIGRANTS from Ireland, Germany, Italy, and eastern European countries arrived on the shores of America with hope in their hearts. Crowded onto ships, clutching all their worldly belongings, they had journeyed across the turbulent Atlantic Ocean. After days, even weeks, at sea, they had at last steamed into New York Harbor, where the Statue of Liberty's torch, held high, seemed to light their way.

Many immigrants encountered hostility, even hatred, as they poured onto Ellis Island and other ports of entry on the eastern seaboard. They were considered inferior, sometimes less than human, by native-born Americans. Torn from the familiar surroundings of "the old country," most immigrants found themselves in a strange, often terrifying land where they had few relatives and friends—or no one at all. Because they did not know the language and the ways of the New World, it was assumed that they were mute or ignorant. Yet in truth these immigrants had great strength of body and mind. Through intelligence and hard work, they were

Immigrants dreamed of the day when they would become citizens of the United States. They completed paperwork and studied hard to pass the citizenship test.

determined to make a better life for themselves and their children. In America, the streets might not be paved in gold, as they had been told, but this was still the "land of opportunity." They knew that they could overcome any obstacle, including devastating poverty and rank discrimination, if only they had a chance.

In the old country, people had few, if any, civil liberties. Many people had suffered terrible persecution. So many immigrants also came to America to escape the tyranny of the Old World. They marveled that Americans were allowed to express their views freely in politics and the arts, as well as in daily conversation. They yearned to become American citizens themselves someday. In a 1923 short story titled "America and I," Anzia Yezierska wrote, "I arrived in America. My young, strong body, my heart and soul pregnant with the unlived lives of generations clamoring for expression."

Many immigrants made their way from the Atlantic coast to the mines and factories of Pennsylvania, Ohio, and other industrial states. Some journeyed to the prairies and distant mountains, where they found work in small towns and on farms as far away as Texas, Montana, and Oregon. However, over the course of a century, hundreds of thousands settled in New York, Philadelphia, Chicago, and other large, growing cities. Having nowhere else to

live, they moved into their own poor neighborhoods, where they crowded into rundown buildings known as tenements.

A tenement is a multifamily dwelling with several apartmentlike living quarters. Derived from the Latin word *tenere* and Medieval Latin word *tenementum*, meaning "to hold," the word was gradually adopted into Medieval French and then into English. Throughout the nineteenth century, tenements were built in the British Isles, including Wales and Ireland. In the United States, immigrants usually lived—and often worked—in tenements in New York and other

Around 1889, this family struggled to survive in the two small, dark rooms of their rat-infested tenement. The father earned just five dollars a week as a coal heaver unloading ships in New York Harbor.

This small kitchen of a working family includes little more than a sink and stove. The doorway leads to a small windowless bedroom in the back of the flat, where several people slept.

large cities. In these buildings, the tenants, or inhabitants, rented small apartments that came to be known as flats. All tenement neighborhoods shared the quandary of too many people crowded into too little space. Of all the tenement neighborhoods, the Lower East Side of New York became a powerful symbol of the struggle of all immigrants.

Usually made of brick, with stone trim around the windows and doors, early tenements were built side by side on narrow lots. Typically, each lot was just twenty-five feet wide and one hundred feet long. With little or no space between the jumble of buildings and few windows, tenements were dark and airless. From their quar-

Tenement dwellers were fortunate if they had one or two windows in their flats. Overlooking the fire escape in the back, this window allows at least a little light to filter into one of the bedrooms.

ters, inhabitants scarcely ever felt the warmth of the sun, drew a breath of fresh air, or glimpsed the sky overhead. Flats in the back rooms of the building were the darkest. One woman explained to Jacob Riis, a passionate and energetic reformer of the late 1800s and early 1900s, why she wished to move to a front apartment: "Why, they have the sun in there. When the door is opened the light comes right in your face."

With little space for a yard, front or back, and no parks in the neighborhood, children grew up in a paved landscape of cement, with no trees or grass. "There was no running brook in which children might splash on hot summer days," wrote Sydney Taylor, author of *All-of-a-Kind Family* and other popular children's books about life on the Lower East Side. "But there was the East River. Its waters stretched out wide and darkly green, and it smelt of fish, ships, and garbage." People hung out on the stoop or sidewalks and streets already clogged with people. Everywhere, inside the tenements and out on the streets, the neighborhood was loud, smelly, unclean—and often dangerous.

Nearly all tenants were poor, but the depth of their poverty ranged from the working poor to the utterly destitute who were too old or too young, too ill or too injured, to labor for even a few pennies. Jacob Riis fought tirelessly to bring public attention to the suffering of tenants on the Lower East Side and in other New York neighborhoods. The title of one of his most influential books, *How the Other Half Lives*, is drawn from a saying that "one half of the world does not know how the other half lives." Although unknown

14

These children have gathered at a place known as Mullin's Alley around 1888–1889. With no parks or yards in the neighborhood, alleys, streets, and rooftops were the only places where children could play outside.

to more fortunate people, tenements became a way of life for generations of immigrants.

Similar to a very small apartment, a tenement flat was usually no more than two rooms. One room typically served as kitchen and living space, and the other as a bedroom. Families often set up one

15

People crowded into the narrow back alley, which was often the only place where they could enjoy a little sunlight. Here, several children gather to play while their mothers labor over piles of laundry.

of these rooms as a sweatshop as well. Here, they labored for long hours, sewing clothes or rolling cigars by hand. If they did not work at home, men, women, and children labored in a nearby factory or shop. Many women also worked as store clerks, laundresses, cooks, or waitresses. A dozen or more people, including newly arrived relatives from Europe and boarders who helped pay the rent, often lived in a single flat. Most of the cramped rooms lacked fresh air and light until 1901, when new laws finally required landlords to construct narrow airshafts between the tightly packed buildings.

Every tenement visitor, including the iceman, midwife, and policeman, as well as the inhabitants themselves, had to pass through a front door to enter the building. They made their way down the narrow hallway and up the dim stairwell. Since there were no elevators, the poorest tenants lived in the highest flats and had to climb four or five flights of stairs. Hattie, a character in *The Tenement Writer*, a novel by Ben Sonder about immigration, journeyed with her parents across the Atlantic Ocean, then to the crowded streets of the Lower East Side, where she came to live in a tenement: "The two-room apartment to which her brother brought the family had few windows and only one view. It looked out on the brick wall of the next building. As for smells, there were all too many—the stench from the toilets in the hallway, the odor of cabbage and onions cooking, the steam and soap of clothes being washed and wrung by hand."

In this suffocating atmosphere, children often ventured onto the fire escape or the roof, which became known as the "tar beach." Here they played games while their parents gathered for parties high above the clamor of the streets. During the sweltering heat and humidity of summer, people often slept on the roofs or fire escapes, where they could catch an occasional breeze. Pigeon coops dotted some rooftops, and flocks of the birds swooped through the

*During the summer,
the unventilated rooms
became unbearably hot
and children often sought
refuge out on the fire escape.
Here, several boys have
built a makeshift tent from
sheets and blankets.*

sky, high above the gray buildings. The roofs were also used as pathways by many people—rent collectors, social workers, and salesmen—anyone who wanted to get away from the jostle of people on the crowded sidewalks.

Strung between tenements, clotheslines reflected the lively spirit of the poor immigrants who inhabited the neighborhood. All sorts

On wash day, laundry hangs on clotheslines strung from one tenement building to another on Roosevelt Street.

of clothing, ranging from diapers to dresses, hung in the gritty city air. Tenants occasionally relied on the lines to carry messages or small packages from one building to another, or people simply shouted to one another from an open window. The sidewalks below were crowded with goods and people—some bustling, others watching the world go by. Jacob Riis described one visit to such a neighborhood: "A full mile we have come, through unbroken ranks of tenements with their mighty, pent-up multitudes. Here they seem, with a common impulse, to overflow into the street."

From pushcarts wedged together along the curb on both sides of the street, peddlers sold everything from shoelaces to sour pickles. The delicious odors of roasting chestnuts and steaming sweet potatoes wafted through the streets, mingling with the smells of horse manure and garbage rising from the gutter. Amid the clatter of horses and wagons, bearded men in long overcoats and old women in thick sweaters or shawls called out to passersby about their wares. Crowds of people sifted among the pushcarts and the traffic on the cobblestone streets, which rang with the voices of people speaking German, Yiddish, Italian, and heavily accented English. In *The Tenement Writer*, "Hattie saw dirty bedding hanging from windowsills and garbage cans spilling over with trash." Out on the street, "a jumble of noises filled Hattie's ears. She heard police whistles, peddlers' cries, children's shouts, and the clatter of horses' hooves all at once."

The sights, sounds, and smells of many cultures blended into a lively and colorful way of life on the Lower East Side. This dynamic and vibrant part of New York City was actually composed of several neighborhoods, notably the East Village, Astor Place, Kleindeutschland (Little Germany), Alphabet City, Five Points, Chinatown, Little Italy, and the Bowery. All these neighborhoods were squeezed together on a scrap of land in lower Manhattan just fourteen miles square. The area is bordered on the north by Fourteenth

Street, west to Broadway and Pearl Street, south to Fulton Street, and east to the East River. The Lower East Side underwent dramatic changes over the years. At one time, the area included both the Five Points, the city's worst slum, and Colonnade Row near Astor Place, a very rich neighborhood that was home to the wealthy financier John Jacob Astor and the author Washington Irving. To the south, the Lower East Side bordered the financial district at Fulton Street.

The history of the Lower East Side may be traced back to Native Americans who originally lived on the forested island now known

Wagons and pushcarts line the street on the bend on Mulberry Street, which always bustled with activity. Here, people gathered to buy and sell goods, as well as visit with friends and neighbors.

This map depicts the network of streets on the Lower East Side. The inset on the right shows the location of this area on the island of Manhattan.

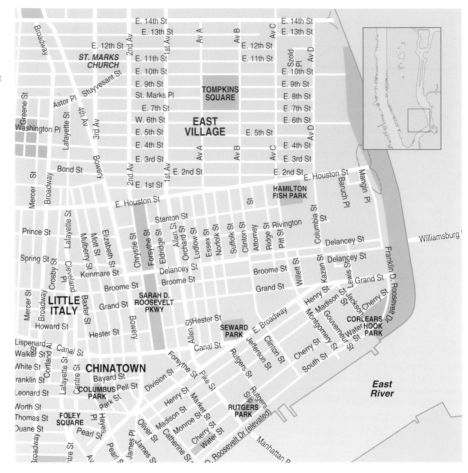

as Manhattan. In the early 1600s, the Dutch West Indies Company established a port and farming colony on the land known as New Amsterdam. In 1664, the British took over the region and New Amsterdam was renamed New York City. Then, after the American Revolution, the state of New York became part of the United States. The city grew rapidly, and by the early 1800s the Lower East Side had already become a thriving hub of factories, with shipyards and slaughterhouses lining the waterfront of the East River. In the days before automobiles and subways, people had to live near their places of work, so the Lower East Side came to be crowded with

working families, including many Irish immigrants and free blacks. At this time, many of these poor people lived in a slum at the Five Points, even as fashionable shops such as Lord & Taylor and Brooks Brothers sprang up on nearby Catherine Street.

In 1833, builders realized that they could profit by constructing small, cheap dwellings for several families, and the first tenement went up on Water Street. Within a few years, tenements had replaced single-family homes and rowhouses in the neighborhood. Between 1845 and 1860, the population of New York City doubled as the city, including the Lower East Side, grew rapidly. Irish immi-

Many of the buildings in Chinatown are reminiscent of the tall, crowded tenements in which immigrants of the nineteenth and early-twentieth centuries made their home on the Lower East Side.

Escaping poverty and perse-cution in Europe, immi-grants from many different countries faced new chal-lenges as they moved into the tightly packed neighborhoods of the Lower East Side.

grants escaped the Potato Famine, and Germans fled civil unrest in the heart of Europe. Immigrants from the Emerald Isle settled throughout the city, but notably in the southern area of the Lower East Side. Germans tended to cluster in a neighborhood north of Division Street that came to be known as Kleindeutschland. Tene-

ments became a quick means of housing the thousands of immi-grants who poured into the Lower East Side.

According to a report to the New York state legislature in 1857, "In its beginning, the tenant house became a real blessing to that class of industrious poor whose small earnings limited their expenses, and whose employment in workshops, stores, or about the warehouses and thoroughfares, render a near residence of much importance." In reality, however, most tenants lived in squalor. In 1862, the superintendent of buildings for the city described tenements as an approach to housing in which "the greatest amount of profit is sought to be realized from the least amount of space, with little or no regard for the health, comfort, or

The family that lived in this tenement sat down to meals in a windowless back room in their small flat. Residents of these dark rooms were often referred to as "cave dwellers."

Candles and oil lamps were the only source of light in early tenements. Here, the solitary flame of an oil lamp manages to illuminate only a small portion of the wall in this rear bedroom.

protection of the lives of the tenants." With no regulations, the construction standards and living conditions of tenements were determined solely by the greed of builders and landlords. A New York State report quoted one landlord's orders to his agent: "Collect the rent in advance, or, failing, eject the occupants."

Early tenements had few windows, and the people who lived in them became known as "cave dwellers." Finally, in 1867, the state of New York passed the reform law known as the Tenement House Act. This legislation defined a tenement as any build-ing "occupied by three or more families, living independently and doing their cooking on the premises; or by more than two families on the floor, so living and cooking and having a common right in the halls, stairways, yards, etc." The law required basic sanitation and health in newly constructed tene-ments, such as at least one outhouse for every twenty people. Thou-sands of windows were cut into interior walls of existing tenements to provide a little ventilation from the hallways or other rooms. However, since the regulations were seldom enforced, this law failed to provide adequate housing for most families packed into dreary flats. According to one follow-up report, "The new tene-ments, that have been recently built, have been usually as badly

Tenement dwellers walked grimy hallways and then often had to climb four or five flights of unlit stairs to reach their flats. The cheaper flats were located on the upper floors.

planned as the old, with dark and unhealthy rooms, often over wet cellars, where extreme overcrowding is permitted."

In 1879, another series of laws required that any new tenement could occupy no more that 65 percent of the 25-by-100-foot lot on which it was built—so people would have a little patch of bare soil for a back yard. Living quarters also had to be better ventilated, with windows opening to a narrow air shaft. They came to be called "dumbbell tenements" because of the shape of their revised floor plans. Despite the good intentions of these regulations, the newly designed buildings did little to improve the plight of tenants, because the Board of Health had no means of enforcing the regulations. High rents, low wages, and little work led to further overcrowding in tenements.

Moreover, between 1880 and 1924, new waves of immigrants flooded into the major cities of the United States, including New York. Many of these immigrants were eastern Europeans and Italians escaping the poverty of their home country and Jews fleeing from persecution in eastern Europe. In just ten years, from 1880 to 1890, 60,000 Jewish immigrants streamed into rundown tenements of the Lower East Side. Most settled in one area of the Lower East Side, which extended from Rivington to Division Streets and from the Bowery to Norfolk Street and came to be known as the Jewish Quarter. The Lower East Side has been described as the Plymouth Rock of Jewish immigrants, who sought to escape the horrors of pogroms in Russia and eastern European countries, just as the Pilgrims had immigrated to America because

of religious persecution in England. By the end of the nineteenth century, the Jewish Quarter had become the most densely populated community on earth.

Yet there was little improvement in living conditions for these waves of newcomers and others who followed. Over time, tenements rose even taller, and the slender gaps between the rows of buildings gradually closed. The Tenement House Commission of 1894 described the double-decker-style tenement, which was often five stories high, as follows: "It is the one hopeless form of tenement construction. It cannot be well ventilated, it cannot be well lighted; it is not safe in case of fire. It is built on a lot 25 feet

Immigrants struggled to keep a few cherished possessions, including photographs, close at hand. These belongings provided a small comfort and helped to remind them of loved ones left behind.

Fire escapes cling to the brick walls of this five-story tenement building on the Lower East Side. The bare metal structures often served as porches where people could enjoy the sunlight and a little fresh air.

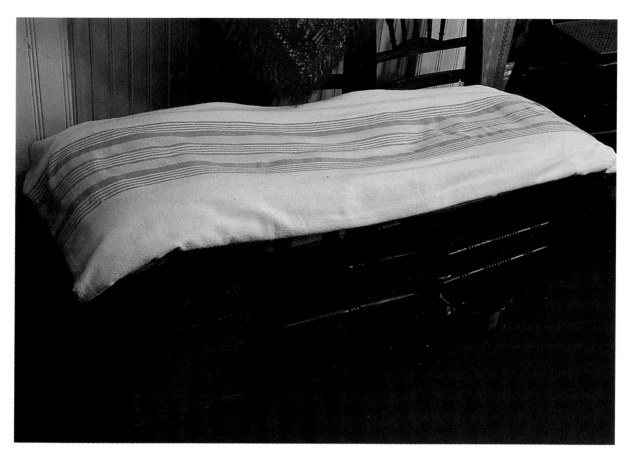

wide and 100 feet or less in depth, with apartments for four families in each story." Here, swarms of immigrants lived and endured many hardships.

The lack of sanitation, in particular, affected the health of tenants. The January 18, 1895, issue of the *New York Times* declared, "That several hundred thousand people in the city have no proper facilities for keeping their bodies clean is a disgrace to the city and to the civilization of the nineteenth century." With no running water and garbage piled high in the street, it was nearly impossible for tenement dwellers to properly bathe and launder clothing. Many people fell victim to diseases that swept through the close

With so many family members squeezed into the two or three small rooms of a flat, people often slept wherever they could find space. Placed on a wooden chest and chairs, this mattress served as a child's bed.

quarters — cholera, typhoid, smallpox, and tuberculosis, which was then known as consumption. In a single year, twenty cases of typhoid were reported in just one house. So many babies died, especially during the hot summers, that the tenements came to be known as "infant slaughterhouses." Jacob Riis wrote, "When the white badge of mourning flutters from every second door, sleepless mothers walk the streets in the gray of early dawn, trying to stir a cooling breeze to fan the brow of the sick baby."

Smallpox and other diseases so ravaged the tenements that teachers in the neighborhood schools had the children recite this saying about how to stay healthy:

I must keep my skin clean,

Wear clean clothes,

Breath pure air,

And live in the sunlight.

Children of all immigrant groups suffered more grievously than anyone. One mother left her baby on the steps of an orphanage with this note: "Take care of Johnny, for God's sake. I cannot." Many abandoned children wandered the streets with no home whatsoever. Along with ragpickers and tramps, they curled up in doorways to sleep at night. According to Jacob Riis, a homeless boy surviving on the street had "all the faults and all the virtues of the lawless life he leads." In his words, "Like rabbits in their burrows, the ragamuffins sleep with at least one eye open." Unable to read or write, these children survived by polishing boots or stealing from

others. There was little to keep these boys off the streets. Their only home had been the tenements, where they had been cursed and beaten so often they had to run away.

Homeless children slept wherever they could find shelter. Barefoot and cold, these boys huddled together for warmth in the corner of an alley near Mulberry Street around 1889.

B Y THE LATE 1800S, MOST TENANTS LABORED IN SWEATSHOPS, either factories in the neighborhood or rooms in their own flats. Usually there were at least two sweatshops on every floor, often as many as four. People earned just pennies for each finished garment—barely enough for food and lodging after long, tedious

Many tenants worked in "sweatshops" at home — and everyone had to work if the family was going to get by. Here, a Jewish family diligently makes clothing in one of the rooms in their flat.

hours of work, six days a week. Nearby factories could be a convenience, but they also posed hazards from pollutants and noise. In factories, the workday was set at ten hours, but in the tenements, labor laws could not be enforced. Men, women, and children worked from daybreak until late into the night, often seven days a week. In the words of Jacob Riis: "Thousands of lighted windows in the tenements glow like dull red eyes in a huge stone wall. From every door multitudes of tired men and women pour forth for a half-hour's rest in the open air before sleep closes the eyes weary

with incessant working. Crowds of half-naked children tumble in the street and on the sidewalk, or doze fretfully on the stone steps."

Young women ironed by the pale light of a window or bent over a sewing machine that whirred from early morning to late at night. The same was true of Bohemian cigarmakers from eastern Europe who represented yet another group of immigrants. Everyone in the family labored for long hours, rolling cigars to be smoked by the wealthy at their leisure. These immigrants received just $3.75 for every thousand cigars, and, working as hard as possible, an entire family could roll only about three thousand cigars a week. While they worked, people went without meals or had a "bite at the bench," usually a small piece of bread or a pickle. If they were lucky, they might have a herring and onion sandwich.

As people labored in the stuffy, unventilated rooms, the heat from the machinery and their own bodies was oppressive. Workers shed not only coats but shirts and sweaters. The tasks were also repetitive and dull, as people bent over their sewing machines and irons, hour after hour. The "sweater," as Jacob Riis called the boss, kept the workers virtually enslaved. He did not wish for his workers to awaken to the injustice of their bondage, so he discouraged them from learning English and paid them so little that they could not rise above their circumstances. Workers were not treated as decently as draft animals, let alone human beings.

DESPITE THE CLOSE QUARTERS AND BAD WORKING CONDITIONS, life was still better than in the old country. In Europe, immigrants and their children, from one generation to the next, were condemned to poverty. In their new home, however, if they worked hard, they might get a better job and apartment. Ultimately, by working long and hard, men managed to support their families and working women proved themselves to be "brave, virtuous, and true," in the words of Jacob Riis. Eventually, through strength, energy, and determination, most immigrants rose above their misery. Many pursued a college education at night after long hours of work, which meant a journey "across the river" in the words of the author Abraham Cahan.

The efforts of Jacob Riis and other social reformers eventually brought widespread public attention to the conditions of poor neighborhoods, including the Lower East Side, which resulted in the Tenement House Law of 1901. This legislation outlawed dumb-

bell tenements and required improvements in existing buildings. For instance, landlords had to provide hallway lighting and install at least one indoor toilet for every two families. A department was also established to enforce the new regulations, although landlords resisted any and all efforts to improve their tenements.

This small room served as both living quarters and bedroom for a family struggling for food, clothing, and shelter. Most people eventually overcame hardships and prospered in the "new country."

In 1910, the population of the Lower East Side peaked at 550,000 people. At the time, across the United States, native-born Americans were reacting negatively to the millions of immigrants pouring into the country. They unjustly blamed crime and other social

The dark hallways and stairs led to several flats on each floor of this building. Each of the doorways opened into a flat where the members of a large family sought to make a home for themselves.

ills on the very people who provided the labor that made the United States wealthy as a nation. Slums came to be viewed as "nurseries of crime." Included among those opposed to immigration were many New Yorkers, such as the author John Van Dyke, who stated arrogantly in the 1909 book *The New New York*, "To the cry of Mr. Riis, 'Abolish the tenements!' there may be suggested an alternative. Why not abolish the tenants?" However, while the very conditions of the tenements may have driven a few desperate people to crime, most immigrants labored to earn an honest living.

By the 1920s, nativists, as opponents to immigration came to be known, managed to stifle the tide of people coming through Ellis Island and other ports of entry when the United States Con-

gress imposed a series of quotas. Only small numbers of carefully selected people from certain foreign countries were now allowed to immigrate to America. Social activists also eventually managed to have thousands of tenements demolished. Streets were widened and parks built in the empty lots. Other tenements succumbed to public works improvements. On the Lower East Side, the most notable construction projects were the Williamsburg and Manhattan bridges, the approaches to which slashed through several neighborhoods.

In 1929, new legislation known as the Multiple Dwellings Law required costly remodeling, including additional bathroom facilities, better ventilation, and fireproofing of existing structures.

Most immigrants had little when they arrived in America. Until they could find suitable work, they often lived out of the suitcases that they had carried on ships across the Atlantic Ocean.

Many tenements were abandoned during the Great Depression when tenants were evicted and landlords simply closed the buildings. These vacant rooms appear haunted, as if awaiting a new life.

However, during the Great Depression, many landlords could not afford to make the upgrades. Instead, they evicted the tenants and closed their buildings. Thousands of flats were left vacant. Later, Mayor Fiorello LaGuardia razed thousands of these tenements and advocated a new solution for sheltering the poor, known as "public housing." Built and managed by city and federal government agencies, public housing offered inexpensive apartments to the poor. In 1934, the first locally built public housing in the United States went up on the Lower East Side. Aptly named First Houses, these dwellings were built on Third Street and Avenue A. However, public housing on the Lower East Side and elsewhere in the United States came to be plagued by overcrowding and many of the other

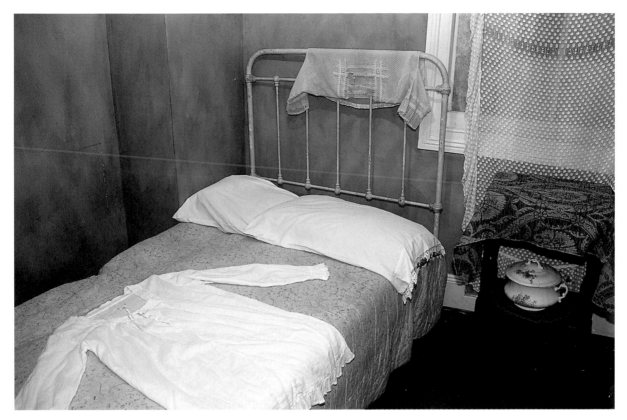

problems of the tenements. In the mid-1940s, following World War II, Puerto Ricans and African Americans began to move to the Lower East Side and settle among older immigrants in the last of the tenements and the new public housing.

In the words of Jacob Riis, "The slum I speak of is our own. We made it." It then became the responsibility of people of good conscience to replace the tenements with more suitable housing.

After World War II, new waves of immigrants settled on the Lower East Side and in other urban neighborhoods across the United States. Like those who had come before them, they sought freedom and prosperity.

THE PEOPLE WHO LIVED IN TENEMENTS WERE HAUNTED BY COLD, poverty, and disease. Yet the tenements and their neighborhoods also afforded a sense of community for friends and family who spoke the same language and had a common cultural heritage, who also shared the common experience of poverty and daily hardship. And, if they could not themselves rise above their poverty, they still worked as peddlers, grocers, and wage earners to give their children a chance for an education and a better life for themselves. Over time, often two or three generations, immigrants overcame seemingly insurmountable obstacles. Tenement life was a hardship, but also a demanding test through which people proved that they had the strength, endurance, and intelligence to eventually prosper in America.

Many often looked back at their years in the tenements with fond memories. The author Sydney Taylor recalled her childhood on the Lower East Side when her own daughter, an only child, was often lonely at bedtime. "I would look around the room with its solitary bed, and my mind would go back to my own childhood. Once again I would be living in the flat on New York's Lower East Side where five little girls shared one bedroom — and never minded bedtime. Snuggled in our beds we would talk and giggle and plan tomorrow's fun and mischief."

Paul Cowan, a reporter for the *Village Voice*, recalled his father's Sunday visits to the old neighborhood on the Lower East Side in his book *An Orphan in History: Retrieving a Jewish Legacy*: "He would spend delighted hours lingering on those crowded, noisy streets, exploring the small stores, watching the transactions, usually in Yiddish, between the shoppers and the storeowners, who wore yarmulkes and stroked long gray beards as they talked. Back then I thought my father liked the neighborhood because it was quaint, or because

he had an insatiable curiosity for new faces, new ideas. It never crossed my mind that the place might evoke memories for him."

In the 1960s, when immigration laws changed and quotas were eliminated, people from other countries again migrated to the Lower East Side, where Irish, Germans, Italians, and Jews had once begun their quest for a better life in the New World. Others in Chinatown and Little Italy continue to make their home in the same crowded neighborhood as previous generations. These recent waves of immigrants are a reminder that most people living in the United States, or one of their ancestors, were once newcomers to this nation. Like those who came before them, they are working to both share in and contribute to the promise of America for their

People continue to live in tenement buildings on the Lower East Side, in Chinatown, and elsewhere across America. Many are newly arrived immigrants, but others have lived in these neighborhoods for generations.

43

children and their grandchildren as expressed in the words of Emma Lazarus inscribed on the Statue of Liberty:

"Give me your tired, your poor,

Your huddled masses yearning to breathe free,

The wretched refuse of your teeming shore.

Send these, the homeless, tempest-tost to me,

I lift my lamp beside the golden door!"

With torch raised, the Statue of Liberty continues to welcome thousands of immigrants to the shores of the United States. The monument still stands as a powerful symbol of hope for all Americans.

FURTHER READING

The following books and Web sites, along with an excellent booklet titled "A Tenement Story: The History of 97 Orchard Street and the Lower East Side Tenement Museum," were consulted in the research for this book.

Basshe, Emanuel Jo. *The Centuries: Portrait of a Tenement House.* 1927. Reprint, Freeport, N.Y.: Books for Libraries Press, 1971.

Day, Jared N. *Urban Castles: Tenement Housing and Landlord Activism in New York City, 1890–1943.* New York: Columbia University Press, 1999.

De Forest, Robert W. *The Tenement House Problem.* 1903. Reprint, New York: Arno Press, 1970.

Diner, Hasia R. *Lower East Side Memories: A Jewish Place in America*. Princeton, N.J.: Princeton University Press, 2000.

Dinwiddie, Emily Wayland. *The Tenants' Manual: A Handbook of Information for Dwellers in Tenement and Apartment Houses and for Settlement and Other Workers*. New York, 1903.

Petty, Alonzo Ray. *Songs of the Tenements and Other Verse*. Andover, N.H.: S. Kelley, 1925.

Reynolds, Marcus T. *The Housing of the Poor in American Cities*. 1893. Reprint, College Park, Md.: McGrath, 1969.

Riis, Jacob A. *The Battle with the Slum*. 1902. Reprint, Montclair, N.J.: Patterson Smith, 1969.

———. *How the Other Half Lives: Studies Among the Tenements of New York*. Cambridge: Belknap Press of Harvard University Press, 1970.

———. *Jacob Riis Revisited: Poverty and the Slum in Another Era*. Garden City, N.Y.: Doubleday, 1968.

———. *A Ten Years' War: An Account of the Battle with the Slum in New York*. Freeport, N.Y.: Books for Libraries Press, 1969.

Veiller, Lawrence. *Housing Reform: A Hand-book for Practical Use in American Cities*. New York: Charities Publication Committee, 1911.

White, Alfred Tredway. *Sun-Lighted Tenements: Thirty-five Years' Experience As an Owner*. New York: National Housing Association, 1912.

CHILDREN'S BOOKS

Granfield, Linda. *97 Orchard Street: Stories of Immigrant Life*.
    Toronto: Tundra Books, 2001.

Sonder, Ben. *The Tenement Writer: An Immigrant's Story*.
    Austin, Tex: Raintree Steck-Vaughn, 1993.

Taylor, Sydney. *All-of-a-Kind Family*. New York: Dell, 1989.
    Other series titles are available in various editions, in-
    cluding *More All-of-a-Kind Family*, *All-of-a-Kind Family
    Downtown*, *All-of-a-Kind Family Uptown*, and *Ella of All-
    of-a-Kind Family*.

SELECTED WEB SITES

ABC News.Com (Tenement Life):
    www.abcnews.go.com/sections/us/dailynews/
    wnt980701_tenement.html.

How the Other Half Lives by Jacob A. Riis:
    www.yale.edu/amstud/inforev/riis/title.html.

Lower East Side Tenement Museum:
    www.tenement.org.

Museum of the City of New York, Jacob Riis Exhibition:
    www.mcny.org/riis.htm.

Channel Thirteen/WNET, Lower East Side Tenement
    Museum: www.wnet.org/tenement.